Switch

to

Holiness

Workbook

12 Actions to be Your Best

Dr. Amanda Goodson

™

Spiritual
Quick Books

ISBN-13:978-0692200872

ISBN-10:0692200878

Printed in the U.S.A.

Second Edition

Switch

to

Holiness

Workbook

12 Actions to be Your Best

Dr. Amanda Goodson

TM

Spiritual
QuickBooks

Acknowledgements:

Thanks to my loving husband who has stood by me and supported by dreams. To my family, I love you dearly.

Special thanks to my spiritual family and friends for all of your support.

I especially thank Rosalyn, Je're, Rosalind and Diane for your encouragement.

TABLE OF CONTENTS

INTRODUCTION

Welcome in the mighty Name of Christ Jesus, our Lord! Are you looking to have a more intimate relationship with God on a daily basis? Looking to live a more fulfilling life separate from the norm? This workbook will serve as a great resource to augment and enhance your learning while reading the "*Switch to Holiness*" book. This workbook will also provide you with valuable insightful exercises to switch from a place of beginning to a place of richness in Christ.

As mentioned in the companion "*Switch to Holiness*" book, people who to holiness make a conscious decision to be better in serving in a place of purpose. People who make the switch are convinced of the power and position that holiness carries. They understand that they have spiritual authority, and they recognize the importance and influence that the Name of Jesus Christ carries. Jesus has all authority over heaven and earth. He delegated authority to His followers and co-laborers to finish His work on earth and in the spiritual realm.

The power to carry out our all our assignments are done through the Holy Spirit. Holiness gives us the ability to be who God created us to be and to live a life far above expectations to a place of peace and authority to make disciples through the Name of Jesus. Holiness sets us apart for service and community.

This workbook, written by Dr. Amanda Goodson will serve as a great tool for churches, nonprofit organizations, groups and spiritual leaders to document strategy, goals and action steps to lead to a better life in Christ. Enjoy working through this inspiring workbook, start being your absolute best, and make the decision to: "*Switch to Holiness*"!

CHAPTER 1

Assess Your Domain Space

"Your current domain space and future sphere of influence are created by perceptions."
- *Dr. Amanda H. Goodson*

"The Spirit of the Lord God is upon Me, because the LORD has anointed Me to preach good tidings to the poor; He has sent Me to heal the brokenhearted, to proclaim liberty to the captives, and the opening of the prison to those who are bound; to proclaim the acceptable year of the LORD, and the day of vengeance of our God; to comfort all who mourn, to console those who mourn in Zion, to give them beauty for ashes , the oil of joy for the spirit of heaviness; that they may be called trees of righteousness; the planting of the LORD, that He may be glorified."
(Isaiah 61:1-3)

CHAPTER 1
ASSESS YOUR DOMAIN SPACE

WHAT IS YOUR DOMAIN SPACE?

A domain space is a place of influence, a realm, a thought, a sphere of action, or even a territory that you govern. It is also a range of personal knowledge and responsibility that is characterized by a region over which you have influence or spiritual ownership.

Domain space is the space where you are currently standing, sitting, working, worshipping and living and where you would influence the things around you. It is also a place where you influence others around you, or over which you have some level of authority or impact. This is a place that can be a way of thinking, it can be a range of personal knowledge, or it can be a physical territory over which you have control.

WHY IS YOUR DOMAIN SPACE SO IMPORTANT?

Your domain space is important because when you have a full awareness of the territory that you govern, and you are living your life in holiness and in accordance to the promises of God, you are able to enjoy rich fellowship with God and have *full* assurance of His blessings.

HOW DO YOU UNDERSTAND YOUR DOMAIN SPACE?

1. Recognize the way the Holy Spirit is in operation within you.

2. Have a full awareness of your strengths, potential differences, advantages, creative gifts and emerging threats surrounding your domain space.

3. Perceive what your domain space is, within your current state or position.

4. Understand your domain space as you perceive what it will be in your future state.

5. Assess and perceive your current opportunities and how they can be utilized as future strengths.

6. Identify what the ultimate ministry assignment is for you based upon this assessment.

DOMAIN SPACE EXERCISE #1:

How do you see yourself right now?

In the boxes below, write your perceived SPACE based on your experience, attitude and performance feedback. Use an extra sheet of paper for this exercise if needed.

Perceived Strengths *(what you do well, right now, with little effort)*	
Perceived Differences and Potential Development areas *(what you do that is different from others and what needs to get improved)*	
Perceived Advantages *(what are the opportunities around you)*	
Perceived Creativity *(what are your creative gifts that need to be used in your current assignment)*	
Perceived Emerging Threats *(what are the threats around you – if you do not get better, what will happen)*	

DOMAIN SPACE EXERCISE #2:

How do your leaders and/or accountability partners see you right now?

In the boxes below, write the your perceived SPACE based on your experience, attitude and performance feedback. Use an extra sheet of paper for this exercise, if needed.

Perceived Strengths *(what you do well, right now, with little effort)*	
Perceived Differences and Potential Development areas *(what you do that is different from others and what needs to get better)*	
Perceived Advantages *(what are the opportunities around you- what needs to get better)*	
Perceived Creativity *(what are your creative gifts that need to be used in your current assignment)*	
Perceived Emerging Threats *(what are the threats around you – if you do not get better, what will happen)*	

In the space below, list any common themes that you notice between what you say about yourself and what others say about you:

1.
2.
3.
4.
5.
6.

In the space below, list why there were common themes, or why not:

DOMAIN SPACE EXERCISE #3:

In the space below, write your perceived ultimate ministry goal. Give your best answer based upon your passion, excitement, desire to make things better, and drive for excellence:

1.
2.
3.
4.
5.

Why did you list this ministry goal?

1.
2.
3.
4.
5.

Who would benefit from you operating in this area of ministry?

1.
2.
3.
4.
5.

What is it about this ministry that others will not do, cannot do, or are not doing at all?

1.
2.
3.
4.
5.

List a time when you were very successful in ministry.

1.
2.
3.
4.
5.

What was different about you that caused you to succeed?

    1.

    2.

    3.

    4.

    5.

Describe a time when you felt like you needed to make a difference in your ministry but did not take the opportunity to do so?

    1.

    2.

    3.

    4.

    5.

List any ministry experience, education or training you have had below. Use this learning throughout this process:

DOMAIN SPACE EXERCISE #4:

Envision that you are in ministry and in alignment with your passion or in the place where you can make a difference. How do you see yourself in this future position?

In the boxes below, write the your perceived SPACE based on your experience, attitude and performance feedback. Use an extra sheet of paper for this exercise if needed.

Perceived Strengths (what you do well, in the future, with little effort)	
Perceived Differences (what you will do that is different from others)	
Perceived Advantages (what advantages do you have)	
Perceived Creativity (what are your creative gifts that need to be used in your future assignment)	
Perceived Emerging Threats (what are the threats around you – if you don't get better, what will happen)	

DOMAIN SPACE EXERCISE #5:

How do your leaders and others in ministry see you in this future position?

In the boxes below, write the your perceived SPACE based on your experience, attitude and performance feedback. Use an extra sheet of paper for this exercise if needed.

Perceived Strengths (what you do well, in the future, with little effort)	
Perceived Differences (what you will do that is different than others)	
Perceived Advantages (what advantages do you have)	
Perceived Creativity (what are your creative gifts that need to be used in your future assignment)	
Perceived Emerging Threats (what are the threats around you – if you don't get better, what will happen)	

List below anything in common between what you say about yourself and what others say about you:

1.
2.
3.
4.
5.
6.

List below why there were common themes, or why not:

DOMAIN SPACE EXERCISE #6:

Acknowledging Talents

On the lines below, list (with detailed description) the specific unique talents and gifts you possess that others have commented back to you and, that have made the ministry within which you serve increase productivity, reach goals or created wins for the organization. Also, list any unique gifts you have outside of ministsry (i.e. drummer, play volleyball, chess champion, etc.)

UNIQUE TALENTS AND GIFTS:

GIFT 1 : _____

_____

_____

_____

GIFT 2 : _____

_____

_____

_____

GIFT 3: _____

_____

_____

_____

GIFT 4: _____

_____

_____

_____

_____

CHAPTER 2

Identify Your Current Spiritual Reality

"For you formed my inward parts; You covered me in my mother's womb. I will praise You, for I am fearfully and wonderfully made; marvelous are Your works, and that my soul knows very well. My frame was not hidden from You, when I was made in secret, and skillfully wrought in the lowest parts of the earth."

(Psalm 139:13-15)

CHAPTER 2
IDENTIFY YOUR CURRENT SPIRITUAL REALITY

WHAT IS YOUR CURRENT SPIRITUAL REALITY?

Your current spiritual reality is found in how you view yourself and is a factor in what shapes your life. Your perspective affects the way you spend your time and money, how you use your talents, and how you value your relationships. Being able to identify your current spiritual reality is knowing where you are spiritually, physically and mentally.

WHY IS YOUR CURRENT SPIRITUAL REALITY IMPORTANT?

Your current spiritual reality is important because we were all specifically created and designed to make a difference in the earth realm. We were created, not only to add life to the earth, but also to give something back. What is important to know in being able to be all that God has created you to do, is to remember that God deserves your best. Trying to serve God in areas where you are not committed to Him is like trying to fit a square peg into a round hole. The longer you try to push to force it or make it fit, the more frustrating and irritating it becomes; and what you produce may have limited results.

HOW DO YOU UTILIZE YOUR CURRENT SPIRITUAL REALITY IN THE KINGDOM?

1. Start with asking yourself how others would perceive you in your place of employment, at home, in the community, or in church. What would others say are your strengths and weaknesses?

2. Have an understanding of the different temperaments and personality types that exist.

3. Once you have identified your current spiritual reality, then you will be able to discover the talents and passions that will transform your life.

4. Develop ideas for the best position that will allow you to leverage your strengths, differences and opportunities.

5. Mitigate, manage or eliminate your threats.

CURRENT SPIRITUAL REALITY EXERCISE #1:

1. **Identify your current spiritual reality, and list 3-5 expected goals within this reality, and write them down below.**

_____

_____

_____

Expected Goal #1: _____

_____

_____

Expected Goal #2: _____

_____

_____

Expected Goal #3: _____

_____

_____

Expected Goal #4: _____

_____

_____

Expected Goal #5: _____

_____

_____

2. **Describe the expected outcome of the goals you have established in this reality and why you believe that this outcome should have such a great ending.**

Expected Outcome #1: _____

_____

Expected Outcome #2: _____

_____

_____

Expected Outcome #3: _____

_____

_____

Expected Outcome #4: _____

_____

_____

Expected Outcome #5: _____

_____

_____

3. **Ask yourself why you are successful and why is this reality is so important. Document your answer below:**

CURRENT SPIRITUAL REALITY EXERCISE #2:

The Right Tools

A. Make a list of what you believe are your dominant gifts and/or talents, and indicate whether or not you are currently serving in that capacity within your current position of ministry.

    1.

    2.

    3.

    4.

    5.

B. Make a list of what you believe are your subordinate gifts and/or talents, and indicate whether or not you are currently serving in that capacity in your current position of ministry.

    1.

    2.

    3.

    4.

    5.

C. If you are currently serving in an area of ministry where your subordinate gifts and/or talents are being utilized rather than where you believe your dominant gifts and/or talents should be utilized, make an assessment of your successes (or failures) in the area below, and describe how you can begin to be utilized to the fullest in the place of your greatest anointing.

_____

_____

_____

_____

_____

CHAPTER 3

Implement Reverse Planning

"We can look into the rearview mirror and see what is behind us; hindsight gives a great view."
- Dr. Amanda H. Goodson

"Finally, brethren, whatever things are true, whatever things are noble, whatever things are just, whatever things are pure, whatever things are lovely, whatever things are of good report, if there is any virtue and if there is anything praiseworthy – meditate on these things."
(Philippians 4:8)

CHAPTER 3
IMPLEMENT REVERSE PLANNING

WHAT IS REVERSE PLANNING?

Reverse planning is the process where you determine a long-term target. Imagine yourself at that point, and then once there, imagine yourself at the point just before you reach your goal. Then imagine yourself at the point just before you reach that goal. Continue this process backwards until you reach the point where you are now. Now you have a plan with clearly defined targets along the way. All you need to do is reverse the plan and carry it out.

WHY IS UNDERSTANDING REVERSE PLANNING IMPORTANT?

Reverse planning is important to help you to identify things you may have missed. With our minds extended and knowing the end of the story, we have a mental image of the end and we know how to plan to reach the destination that God has set for us. When we visualize what God says about us and get a clear mental picture of who we are, and then we can translate that into action steps that we can take right now.

HOW DO YOU IDENTIFY AND ADAPT TO REVERSE PLANNING?

You identify and adapt to Reverse Planning by doing the following:

1. Define your goals.

2. Identify the steps and sequence needed to achieve your goals.

3. Create a deadline-driven timeline by committing your plan to a specific time line.

4. Seek support.

Let's determine how you would implement reverse planning in the exercises below.

REVERSE PLANNING EXERCISE #1:

God has a specific purpose, future and destiny for your life. Envision what that purpose, future and destiny looks like to you. In the space below, give a detailed description of what you believe is that purpose, future and/or destiny and how you believe it will be fulfilled.

Using the process of Reverse Planning, list up to ten (10) steps in the reverse action plan that can be used to fulfill that area of purpose and/or service.

    10.

    9.

    8.

    7.

    6.

    5.

    4.

    3.

    2.

    1.

For each of the steps listed above, describe what step(s) should be taken to get on track (make a list).

Step 1: _____

_____

Step 2: _____

_____

_____

Step 3: _____

_____

_____

Step 4: _____
_____
_____

Step 5: _____
_____
_____

Step 6: _____
_____
_____

Step 7: _____
_____
_____

Step 8: _____
_____
_____

Step 9: _____
_____

Step 110: _____
_____
_____

Ask yourself why you believe this action plan will be successful. Document your answers below:

REVERSE PLANNING EXERCISE #2:

Make a list of your successes and gains in this plan:

Make a list of the ways you overcame challenges, obstacles and barriers:

1. **Define your goal**
   a. What do you want to accomplish?
   b. Define your goal as specifically as possible. Ask yourself why it is important and points to Christ Jesus.

2. **Identify the steps and sequence needed to achieve your goals.**
    a. Write out a random list of all the steps and resources that you need to accomplish your goal.
    b. Estimate the time and resources (money and people) you need to complete each step on the list.
    c. Group the random steps into clusters and sequence them.
    d. Think about creating a starting outline to begin the sequencing.

3. **Create a deadline-driven timeline by committing your plan to paper and calendar by assigning specific due dates to each major goal and supporting steps.** *It is much easier to create your calendar by working backwards – keeping the end in mind.*

4. **Seek support.**
    a. Get more feedback or input from someone to make sure you aren't overlooking something critical.
    b. Check to see if identified resources are available.
    c. Reverse planning can give you confidence as you move forward toward achieving your goal.

REVERSE PLANNING EXERCISE#3:

In the space below, list five individuals (i.e., mentors, accountability partners, or people who have spoken into your life) to whom you have planned to communicate your plan. Indicate the statement that you will use to present your vision, and also set up a reward system for success. Is there anything you need to change?

Person #1. Statements to use - Start your statmement with "My desire is to…."

_____

_____

_____

_____

_____

_____

How did this person respond to your statements?:_____

_____

_____

_____

_____

What do you need to change, and how will you hold yourself accountable?:_____

_____

_____

_____

_____

_____

Person #2. Statements to use - Start your statmement with "My desire is to…."

_____

_____

_____

_____

_____

_____

How did this person respond to your statements?:_____

_____

_____

_____

_____

What do you need to change, and how will you hold yourself accountable?:_____

_____

_____

_____

_____

Person #3. Statements to use - Start your statmement with "My desire is to…."

_____

_____

_____

_____

_____

_____

How did this person respond to your statements?:_____

_____

_____

_____

_____

_____

What do you need to change, and how will you hold yourself accountable?: _____

_____

_____

_____

_____

_____

Person #4. Statements to use- Start your statmement with "My desire is to…."

_____

_____

_____

_____

_____

_____

How did this person respond to your statements?:_____

_____

_____

_____

_____

_____

What do you need to change, and how will you hold yourself accountable?: _____

_____

_____

_____

_____

_____

Person #5. Statements to use- Start your statmement with "My desire is to…."

_____

_____

_____

_____

_____

_____

How did this person respond to your statements?:_____

_____

_____

_____

_____

What do you need to change, and how will you hold yourself accountable?:_____

_____

_____

_____

_____

_____

CHAPTER 4

Develop and Deploy Kingdom Action Steps

"Launch your differences to make a difference."
- Dr. Amanda H. Goodson

"But as He who called you is holy, you also be holy in all your conduct, because it is written, 'Be holy, for I am holy'."
(1 Peter 1:15-16)

CHAPTER 4
DEVELOP AND DEPLOY KINGDOM ACTION STEPS

HOW DO I DEVELOP AND DEPLOY KINGDOM ACTION STEPS?

The development and deployment of Kingdom action steps requires a conscious effort toward holiness thinking. This thinking should be extended to a specific situation where you become ready to act on the plan of holiness.

WHY IS DEVELOPMENT AND DEPLOYMENT OF KINGDOM ACTIONS STEPS IMPORTANT?

The development and deployment of Kingdom action steps is important because we are called to be holy because the God we serve is a holy God, and we were created in His image and likeness. Holiness is not so much about how you appear to others, but rather where you are actually headed. There is a definite path of holiness (a narrow path), and it is up to each of us to consciously be willing to walk that path on a daily basis.

HOW DO YOU DEVELOP AND DEPLOY KINGDOM ACTION STEPS?

1. Recognize that it is the Holy Spirit that gives you the power and energy you need in order to walk the path of holiness on a daily basis.

2. Release your mind-set of excellence and allow your new thinking to push you to a place of victory.

3. Identify the best you and the best time for you to excel.

4. Identify what promotes the holiness actions that will be seen as powerful.

5. Adjust to your new distinction of holiness in order to advance the mission of the Kingdom of God, as well as establishing a standard for others to replicate.

DEVELOPING AND DEPLOYING KINGDOM ACTION STEPS EXERCISE #1:

Power and Energy

In the spaces below, write down 3-5 ways that the Holy Spirit gives you total energy and how it makes you feel.

1. _____

_____

_____

_____

_____

_____

2. _____

_____

_____

_____

_____

_____

3. _____

_____

_____

_____

_____

_____

4. _____

5.

DEVELOPING AND DEPLOYING KINGDOM ACTION STEPS EXERCISE #2:

Attitude

In the spaces below, write down 3-5 ways that the development and deployment of a Kingdom action attitude can shift you to becoming more successful, and why is it important to have that attitude now.

1. _____

_____

_____

_____

_____

_____

2. _____

_____

_____

_____

_____

_____

3. _____

_____

_____

_____

_____

_____

4. _____

_____

_____

_____

_____

_____

5. _____

_____

_____

_____

_____

_____

DEVELOPING AND DEPLOYING KINGDOM ACTION STEPS
EXERCISE #3:

Convergence

In the spaces below, write down 3-5 ways you can enjoy walking in holiness and have great power and energy doing it.

1. _____

_____

_____

_____

_____

_____

2. _____

_____

_____

_____

_____

_____

3. _____

_____

_____

_____

_____

_____

4. _____

_____

_____

5. _____

44

DEVELOPING AND DEPLOYING KINGDOM ACTION STEPS
EXERCISE #4:

In the boxes below, write down 3-5 people to whom you are willing to mentor or to become an accountability partner. How will you assist in the transformation of their mind-set in order to become successful?

1. _____

_____

_____

_____

_____

_____

2. _____

_____

_____

_____

_____

_____

3. _____

_____

_____

_____

_____

_____

4. _____

_____

_____

_____

5. _____

CHAPTER 5

Adapt to a Kingdom Character

"After we are off the launch pad, we operate in an open space."
-Dr. Amanda H. Goodson

"Then God said, 'Let Us make man in Our image, according to Our likeness; let them have dominion over the fish of the sea, over the birds of the air, and over the cattle, over all the earth and over every creeping thing that creeps on the earth.' So God created man in His own image; in the image of God He created him; male and female He created them. Then God blessed them, and God said to them, 'Be fruitful and multiply; fill the earth and subdue it; have dominion over the fish of the sea, over the birds of the air, and over every living thing that moves on the earth'."
(Genesis 1:26-28)

"…Not by might nor by power, but by My Spirit, says the LORD of hosts."
(Zechariah 4:6)

CHAPTER 5
ADAPT TO A KINGDOM CHARACTER

HOW DO YOU ADAPT TO A KINGDOM CHARACTER?

You adapt to a Kingdom character by understanding that God made everything for His glory. He made us in His image (spiritual nature) and likeness (functionality) to rule over the earth. He put the man and woman in charge of everything that He made, and He gave them the ability to have dominion.

The Holy Spirit serves as our Teacher, our Revealer, our Counselor, and He will give us wisdom, understanding, and might to do the task. It is not by our power or by our might, but all things can, and should, be done by the Holy Spirit over all the armies of heaven and earth.

WHY IS ADAPTING TO A KINGDOM CHARACTER IMPORTANT?

Adapting to a Kingdom character is important because the Word of God compels us to pray that His Kingdom agenda permeate the earth. We play a vital role as partakers and partners with Christ in making this happen.

HOW DO YOU ADAPT TO A KINGDOM CHARACTER?

1. Pray for God's agenda, in agreement with others, to be implemented and planted firmly in the earth, and understand that you must come to the new birth through Jesus Christ.

2. Be willing to choose the path of inspiration in order to inspire others; no matter where that path may lead.

3. Have the resolve to take a stand for God; in spite of obstacles and oppositions.

4. Identify others that may benefit from this success.

5. Make a record of what is not working, apply course correction, and use this information in the future.

6. Solicit support from others to help where necessary.

7. Re-calibrate your position using your strengths and differences to catapult the organization forward.

8. Gather different perspectives and apply them creatively.

KINGDOM CHARACTER EXERCISE #1:

Inspiring Others

In the space below, list 3-5 ways in which you are currently working to be able to inspire others. Also in the space below, list the ministry projects that are going well and tell why . List what is not going well and tell why.

Project #1. _____

_____

What is working well and why: _____

_____

What is not working well and why: _____

_____

Project #2. _____

_____

What is working well and why: _____

_____

What is not working well and why: _____

_____

Project #3. _____

_____

What is working well and why: _____

_____

What is not working well and why: _____

_____

Project #4. _____

_____

What is working well and why: _____

_____

What is not working well and why: _____

_____

Project #5. _____

_____

What is working well and why: _____

_____

What is not working well and why: _____

_____

KINGDOM CHARACTER EXERCISE #2:

Look carefully at your list from the previous exercise and determine if you can make course corrections to what is and what is not working well. Identify what is impeding the progress of these methods, and use your reverse planning strategy to re-write your plan below:

_____

_____

_____

_____

_____

_____

_____

_____

_____

_____

KINGDOM CHARACTER EXERCISE #3:

Accountability Partner Participation

In the space below, list the accountability partners, for your ministry projects, that you need to help you to re-calibrate your thinking.

ACCOUNTABILITY PARTNERS AND THEIR COMMENTS:

Project #1. _____

_____

What is working well and why: _____

_____

What is not working well and why: _____

_____

Project #2. _____

_____

What is working well and why: _____

_____

What is not working well and why: _____

_____

Project #3. _____

_____

What is working well and why: _____

_____

What is not working well and why: _____

_____

Project #4. _____

_____

What is working well and why: _____

What is not working well and why: _____

_____

Project #5. _____

_____

What is working well and why: _____

_____

What is not working well and why: _____

_____

CHAPTER 6

Exercise your Authority

"What gives lift should create alignment with personality and purpose."
- Dr. Amanda H. Goodson

"You will also declare a thing, and it will be established for you; so light will be established on your ways."

(Job 22:28)

CHAPTER 6
EXERCISE YOUR AUTHORITY

WHAT IS EXERCISING YOUR AUTHORITY?

Exercising your authority is always knowing that there is nothing more powerful than the spoken Word. Through faith, you can choose to change your life and exercise the authority that God has already placed in you. Furthermore, understanding the principle of how the world was framed from the beginning, without a thing first being conceived in the mind and then being spoken out – without calling those things that are not as though they were (Romans 4:17) – nothing that currently exists would exist.

WHY IS EXERCISING YOUR AUTHORITY SO IMPORTANT?

Exercising your authority is important because to be able to activate and operate within the full anointing of God, you must first understand that all the necessary resources are already at your disposal. The presence of the Holy Spirit makes this evident, and praying and asking for what you want in Jesus' Name places His power and glory in the forefront.

HOW DO YOU UNDERSTAND EXERCISING YOUR AUTHORITY?

1. List ways in which you can harness and maximize the potential of your thoughts and words.

2. List ways you express acknowledgement and appreciation of the authority of others.

3. List how you leveraged your differences to make a difference.

4. Plan how you will adapt your current state into your future.

5. Develop a way to continue to use this process routinely.

EXERCISE YOUR AUTHORITY EXERCISE #1:

What is your definition of authority?

Authority is:

_____

_____

_____

_____

_____

_____

In the space below, list 3-5 ways to exercise your spiritual authority.

1.
2.
3.
4.
5.

EXERCISE YOUR AUTHORITY EXERCISE #2:

Authority Acknowledgement

List unique ways to express acknowledgement and appreciation for the authority of others around you in the space below.

    1.

    2.

    3.

    4.

    5.

Respect and Disrespect

In the space below, list ways that respectful behaviors serve as motivation.

    1.

    2.

    3.

    4.

    5.

List ways that disrespectful behaviors can serve as demotivators in the space below.

    1.

    2.

    3.

    4.

    5.

In the space below, write a plan for how you will handle difficulties while exercising your authority and still remaining true to yourself?

_____

_____

_____

_____

_____

_____

_____

_____

_____

_____

In the space below, write a plan for how you will create harmony while exercising your authority and still remaining true to yourself?

_____

_____

_____

_____

_____

_____

_____

_____

_____

_____

CHAPTER 7

Leverage Kingdom Power

"But you shall receive power when the Holy Spirit has come upon you; and you shall be witnesses to Me in Jerusalem, and in all Judea and Samaria, and to the end of the earth."
(Acts 1:8)

CHAPTER 7
LEVERAGE KINGDOM POWER

WHAT IS LEVERAGING YOUR KINGDOM POWER?

Leveraging Kingdom power is learning how to be sanctified and walk in holiness, how to partake of Christ's life, and how to become an overcomer in order to bear righteous fruit.

WHY IS LEVERAGING YOUR KINGDOM POWER IMPORTANT?

God is the source of all power, and he places His rulers in positions of power and rules and controls our destinies by His power. Leveraging Kingdom power is important because, through the power of God, we have the ability to execute the impossible.

HOW DO YOU UNDERSTAND HOW TO LEVERAGE YOUR KINGDOM POWER?

1. List ways that you are able to leverage your Kingdom power.

1. List ways you express acknowledgement and appreciation of the accomplishments of others.

2. List how you leveraged your differences to make a difference.

3. Plan how you will adapt your current state into your future.

4. Develop a way to continue to use this process routinely.

LEVERAGE KINGDOM POWER EXERCISE #1:

The Process of Sanctification

In the space below, write down your definition of sanctification:

_____

_____

_____

_____

_____

_____

In the space below, list 3-5 areas in which you are currently working to live a sanctified life. Also, in the space below, list some of the challenges you face and what you are doing to overcome them.

Area #1. _____

_____

Challenge:_____

_____

_____

How it is overcome: _____

_____

Area #2. _____

_____

Challenge:_____

_____

_____

How it is overcome: _____

_____

Area #3. _____

_____

Challenge:_____

_____

_____

How it is overcome: _____

_____

Area #4. _____

_____

Challenge:_____

_____

_____

How it is overcome: _____

_____

Area #5. _____

_____

Challenge:_____

_____

_____

How it is overcome: _____

_____

LEVERAGE KINGDOM POWER EXERCISE #2:

In the spaces below, write down 3 ways that leveraging Kingdom power can shift you to a place of holiness and to becoming more successful, and why is that important to you at this time:

1. _____

_____

_____

_____

_____

2. _____

_____

_____

_____

_____

3. _____

_____

_____

_____

_____

LEVERAGE KINGDOM POWER EXERCISE #3:

In the space below, list 3-5 approaches that you use in assisting others to develop their ability to leverage Kingdom power by staying cleansed, filled and empowered. Discuss what makes these approaches successful.

Approach #1. _____

_____

_____

_____

_____

_____

_____

Approach #2. _____

_____

_____

_____

_____

_____

_____

_____

Approach #3. _____

_____

_____

_____

_____

_____

_____

Approach #4. _____

_____

_____

_____

_____

_____

_____

Approach #5. _____

_____

_____

_____

_____

_____

_____

CHAPTER 8

Making a Lasting Impact

"Space Language adds power to the conversation within the organization – speak up and be heard."

- Dr. Amanda H. Goodson

"Let your light so shine before men, that they may see your good works and glorify your Father in heaven."

(Matthew 5:16)

CHAPTER 8
MAKING A LASTING IMPACT

HOW DO YOU MAKE A LASTING IMPACT?

Making a lasting impact is first accomplished by discovering what true gifts and talents you possess and what you are passionate about. Once you have developed expertise in that area, your persistent determination and obedience in operating in that area places you in a position where success and impacting others is undeniable.

WHY IS MAKING A LASTING IMPACT SO IMPORTANT?

Many in the world are searching for something greater than themselves. Making a lasting impact is important for the people of God because it gives them the opportunity to demonstrate to the world that something else is available. The walk of holiness and assurance in who, and in whose, you are places you in a position of influence.

HOW DO YOU UNDERSTAND HOW TO MAKE A LASTING IMPACT?

1. Identify what is my current position.

2. Know where I stand with God.

3. Recognize the gifts and talents that I have to work with and where I desire them to take me.

4. Identify how to get there from here.

5. Understand how to use those gifts and talents to impact others.

MAKING A LASTING IMPACT EXERCISE #1:

Impacting Others

As a royal priest, you are called to be salt and light to the world. Your ability to effectively impact others requires a mature relationship with God. Make a list of the places where you believe you would have the greatest impact on others.

1.

2.

3.

4.

5.

6.

7.

8.

9.

10.

MAKING A LASTING IMPACT EXERCISE #2:

In the space below, list 3-5 areas in which you are currently working to be able to impact others. Also in the space below, list those that are going well and tell why. List what is not going well and tell why.

Area #1. _____

_____

What is working well and why: _____

_____

What is not working well and why: _____

Area #2. _____

_____

What is working well and why: _____

_____

What is not working well and why: _____

Area #3. _____

_____

What is working well and why: _____

_____

What is not working well and why: _____

Area #4. _____

_____

What is working well and why: _____

_____

What is not working well and why: _____

Area #5. _____

_____

What is working well and why: _____

_____

What is not working well and why: _____

MAKING A LASTING IMPACT EXERCISE #3:

Look carefully at your responses from the previous exercise, and determine if you can make any impactful corrections to what is not working well. Identify what is impeding your ability to make a lasting impact, and discuss how you will be able to effectively make any corrections by utilizing the reverse planning strategy learned in Chapter 3.

Correction #1:_____

_____

_____

_____

_____

Correction #2:_____

_____

_____

_____

_____

Correction #3:_____

_____

_____

_____

_____

Correction #4:_____

_____

_____

_____

_____

Correction #5:_____

_____

_____

_____

_____

CHAPTER 9

Align Your Kingdom Compass

"However, when He, the Spirit of truth, has come, He will guide you into all truth; for He will not speak on His own authority, but whatever He hears He will speak; and He will tell you things to come."
(John 16:13)

CHAPTER 9
ALIGN YOUR KINGDOM COMPASS

WHAT IS ALIGNING YOUR KINGDOM COMPASS?

Your Kingdom compass is the direct and true alignment with the order of God. Aligning your Kingdom compass is being in the place where you are able to fulfill the intended mission and purpose of God.

WHY IS ALIGNING YOUR KINGDOM COMPASS SO IMPORTANT?

Aligning your Kingdom compass is important because our true alignment assures us of full power, potential, and lasting energy. Through our love for God, we are able to endure. It is that endurance that guarantees us the crown of life.

HOW DO YOU UNDERSTAND ALIGNING YOUR KINGDOM COMPASS?

1. Ask for wisdom for direction in every area of your life.

2. Commit to follow the wisdom that has been given to you.

3. Live a life with total dependence upon God, remembering His sovereign will.

4. Have the ability to endure trying times with humility and patience.

ALIGN YOUR KINGDOM COMPASS EXERCISE #1:

Determining Your Position

Consider the physical make-up of a compass (a device used to determine geographical direction). When journeying through the many trials and considering the many choices that have to be made daily, in the space below, describe what you currently do to keep yourself aligned in the Kingdom.

_____

_____

_____

_____

_____

_____

Many of today's automobiles are equipped with a GPS system to keep them geographically on track. After personally skirting a particular obstacle in ministry, describe the positioning system that you currently use in order to recalibrate and return to your original course and get yourself back on track.

_____

_____

_____

_____

_____

_____

ALIGN YOUR KINGDOM COMPASS EXERCISE #2:

God's Positioning System (GPS)

A. Keeping yourself aligned in the Kingdom requires listening to the Lord through the workings of His Holy Spirit and being obedient to His leading. In the space below, make a list of tools or things that you currently do or use to keep spiritually in tune with the leading of the Holy Spirit.

1.

2.

3.

4.

5.

6.

7.

8.

9.

10.

B. Understanding that the walk of holiness in the Kingdom will not always be smooth. The steps in following God's Positioning System require:
1. Asking for wisdom
2. Commiting to following God's wisdom
3. Making plans in humility
4. Living your life with dependence upon God
5. Enduring trying times with patience

In the space below, describe your strategy for utilizing these 5 steps in remaining in alignment with the Kingdom. If there is a fork in the road where uncertainty seems to subsist, describe your method for overcoming it.

_____

_____

_____

_____

_____

_____

_____

CHAPTER 10

Achieve Spiritual Position

"Therefore, my beloved brethren, be steadfast, immovable, always abounding in the work of the Lord, knowing that your labor is not in vain in the Lord."

(1 Corinthians 15:58)

CHAPTER 10
ACHIEVE SPIRITUAL POSITION

WHAT IS ACHIEVING SPIRITUAL POSITION?

Achieving spiritual position is having God bestow upon you the special position of Kingdom Priest and being able to represent Him as His ambassador in the earth realm. This position comes by virtue of your ability to walk in holiness, keep His covenants, and be obedient to His Word.

WHY IS ACHIEVING SPIRITUAL POSITIONING SO IMPORTANT?

Achieving spiritual position and being able to walk in holiness is beneficial primarily for the purpose of drawing others to Christ. Through their witness of your achievement of holiness in Christ, they will be encouraged to do the same. Jesus is the true Vine and all who are true believers are the branches. He expects much fruit from His branches.

HOW DO YOU UNDERSTAND HOW TO ACHIEVE SPIRITUAL POSITION?

1. List ways to achieve spiritual positioning.

2. List ways you encourage and acknowledge spiritual positioning in others.

3. List how your spiritual position makes a difference in how you relate to others.

4. Plan how you will assist others in understanding their spiritual position.

5. List ways to continue to grow spiritually and develop a process to be used to provide and to promote positive feedback for others.

ACHIEVE SPIRITUAL POSITION EXERCISE #1:

Spiritual Position Achievement

In the space below, list 3-5 activities you do (or will begin to do) on a daily basis to achieve spiritual position. If there are areas that have not been successful, describe the necessary steps for overcoming the problem and then to become successful.

Activity #1: _____

_____

Overcoming Process: _____

_____

_____

Activity #2: _____

_____

Overcoming Process: _____

_____

_____

Activity #3: _____

_____

Overcoming Process: _____

_____

_____

Activity #4: _____

_____

Overcoming Process: _____

_____

_____

Activity #5: _____

Overcoming Process: _____

_____

_____

ACHIEVE SPIRITUAL POSITION EXERCISE #2:

Spiritual Positioning for Others

Considering your process for achieving spiritual position in the previous exercise, list 3-5 ways you will plan to assist others in achieving their spiritual position.

1.

2.

3.

4.

5.

In the space below, describe in detail how each phase of assisting others will include such things as the following:
1. Meeting their specific needs
2. Offering new perspectives
3. Demonstration of improved confidence
4. Providing constructive feedback
5. Providing new knowledge
6. Encouragement through increased motivation

1. Meeting their specific needs:

_____

_____

_____

_____

2. Offering new perspectives:

_____

_____

_____

_____

3. Demonstration of improved confidence:

_____

_____

_____

_____

4. Providing constructive feedback:

_____

_____

_____

_____

5. Providing new knowledge:

_____

_____

_____

_____

6. Encouragement through increased motivation:

_____

_____

_____

_____

CHAPTER 11

Switch to a Pace of Spiritual Excellence

"I beseech you therefore, brethren, by the mercies of God, that you present your bodies a living sacrifice, holy, acceptable to God, which is your reasonable service. And do not be conformed to this world, but be transformed by the renewing of your mind, that you may prove what is that good and acceptable and perfect will of God.
(Romans 12: 1-2)

CHAPTER 11
SWITCH TO A PACE OF SPIRITUAL EXCELLENCE

WHAT IS A PACE OF SPIRITUAL EXCELLENCE?

A pace of spiritual excellence is the ability to understand and be able to fully operate in the place of purpose. A person operating in this position possesses the quality of being outstanding and has no problem doing what the Lord has called him/her to do, and does it with wisdom and vigor.

WHY IS A PACE OF SPIRITUAL EXCELLENCE SO IMPORTANT?

A pace of spiritual excellence is important because, without it, perfectionism would be established as a basis for how we operate. With perfectionism there is generally no margin for error, which results in the individual placing him/herself in the forefront, thus taking the focus off God.

HOW DO YOU UNDERSTAND A PACE OF SPIRITUAL EXCELLENCE?

1. Describe the things you do that bring glory to God.

2. Develop a mindset for having singleness of purpose with unwavering actions.

3. List the actions that demonstrate alignment with God's plan for your life.

4. Specify the time that is actually spent with the Lord and describe how to maintain a balance between work and rest.

5. Determine to walk in faith and not fear.

6. Choose only to take control of things that are yours to govern, and allow God to control all the things that belong in His hands.

7. Possess excellence of mind, body and spirit, and begin to walk in the Spirit.

ACHIEVE A PACE OF EXCELLENCE EXERCISE #1:

Glorifying God

In the space below, list 3-5 of the most frequently used things you do to bring glory to God.

1. _____

2. _____

3. _____

4. _____

5. _____

In the space below, list 3-5 of the things/areas where you can do more to bring God glory. Describe your plan for increasing the frequency of these items, bringing greater balance to your spiritual life and pace of excellence.

1. _____

Increase frequency by: _____

_____

2. _____

Increase frequency by: _____

_____

3. _____

Increase frequency by: _____

_____

4. _____

Increase frequency by: _____

_____

5. _____

Increase frequency by: _____

_____

ACHIEVE A PACE OF EXCELLENCE EXERCISE #2:

Balance and Excellence

Balance requires weighing and measuring those things that you encounter in life that may offer challenges to you. In the space below, describe your plan and your efforts for achieving and maintaining spiritual balance in terms of the following examples:

A. Weighing Good Versus Bad Relationships
B. Weighing Truth and Error
C. Weighing Good Instruction Against Bad Instruction

A. Good vs. Bad Relationships: _____

_____

_____

_____

_____

_____

_____

_____

B. Truth vs. Error: _____

_____

_____

_____

_____

_____

_____

_____

C. Good vs. Bad Instruction: _____

_____

_____

_____

_____

_____

_____

_____

ACHIEVE A PACE OF EXCELLENCE EXERCISE #3:

Singleness of Purpose

Without murmuring or complaining, Daniel exhibited strong faith and unrelenting devotion to God by refusing to bow down to his oppressors. In the space below, describe how your position in terms of singleness of purpose moves you, or will cause you to move, into a pace of excellence.

_____

_____

_____

_____

_____

_____

_____

_____

_____

_____

_____

_____

_____

_____

CHAPTER 12

Create Spiritual Consonance

"Therefore if there is any consolation in Christ, if any comfort of love, if any fellowship of the Spirit, if any affection and mercy, fulfill my joy by being like-minded, having the same love, being of one accord, of one mind. Let nothing be done through selfish ambition or conceit, but in lowliness of mind let each esteem others better than himself. Let each of you look out not only for his own interests, but also for the interests of others."

(Philippians 2:1-4)

CHAPTER 12
CREATE SPIRITUAL CONSONANCE

WHAT IS SPIRITUAL CONSONANCE?

Spiritual consonance is the ability to connect spiritually to people and is demonstrated through the power that the Lord has given you through prayer, faith, and obedience. Spiritual consonance is manifested through spiritual giftings.

WHY IS SPIRITUAL CONSONANCE SO IMPORTANT?

Spiritual consonance is important because it affords you the ability, desire, and the capacity to perform certain function(s) within the body of Christ. Every believer is born with a variety of talents and gifts, along with divinely inspired spiritual gift(s). The service that each provides involves God the Father, the Son, and the Holy Spirit.

HOW DO YOU UNDERSTAND SPIRITUAL CONSONANCE?

1. Distinguish between motivational, ministry, and manifestation gifts.
2. Study the scriptures and know the Word concerning the gifts.
3. Become equipped to see the needs that are overlooked by others.
4. Strengthen and encourage the body of Christ.

CREATE SPIRITUAL CONSONANCE EXERCISE #1:

Consonance and Gift Distinction

A.   Motivational, ministry and manifestation gifts each distinctly play a key role which, when working together, create spiritual consonance to strengthen and provide encouragement for the body of Christ. Using the chart below, identify what you believe are your spiritual gift(s) and indicate which area demonstrates your dominant gift(s) and which area demonstrates your subordinate gift(s).

Motivational Gifts (Gifts that shape your perspective on life and are motivated by God – characterized by inherent qualities)		Ministry Gifts (Gifts that represent what God uses to meet the needs of the body – ministries and offices of the church)		Manifestation Gifts (Gifts that represent what God does through you – demonstration of the power of the Holy Spirit)	
Dominant	Subordinate	Dominant	Subordinate	Dominant	Subordinate

Motivational Gifts
1. Prophecy
2. Service
3. Teaching
4. Exhortation
5. Giving
6. Administration
7. Mercy

Ministry Gifts
1. Apostle
2. Prophet
3. Evangelist
4. Pastor
5. Teacher

Manifestation Gifts
1. Word of wisdom
2. Word of knowledge
3. Faith
4. Healing
5. Working of miracles
6. Prophecy
7. Discerning of spirits
8. Diverse tongues
9. Interpretation of tongues

CREATE SPIRITUAL CONSONANCE EXERCISE #2:

In the space below, identify 3-5 activities that you will initiate to edify the body on an individual level within your church setting, bringing spiritual consonance and edification to the body.

1.

2.

3.

4.

5.

Describe in detail the plan for initiating each of the activities previously identified.

Details for Plan #1: _____

_____

_____

Details for Plan #2: _____

_____

_____

Details for Plan #3: _____

_____

_____

Details for Plan #4: _____

_____

_____

Details for Plan #5: _____

_____

_____

The church exists in the community. In the space below, identify 3-5 activities that you will initiate to edify the body on a corporate level offering mutual edification to those who have needs that may be overlooked and not be met within the typical church setting.

Details for Plan #1: _____

_____

_____

Details for Plan #2: _____

_____

_____

Details for Plan #3: _____

_____

_____

Details for Plan #4: _____

_____

_____

Details for Plan #5: _____

_____

_____

98

CONCLUSION

"Choose harmony and celebrate the power of personality and purpose each and every day. Others will begin to need and notice your extraordinary ways."

Dr. Amanda H. Goodson

"Finally, brethren, whatever things are true, whatever things are noble, whatever things are just, whatever things are pure, whatever things are lovely, whatever things are of good report, if there is any virtue and if there is anything praiseworthy – meditate on these things. The things which you learned and received and heard and saw in me, these do, and the God of peace will be with you. …I can do all things through Christ who strengthens me."

(Philippians 4:8-9, 13)

Write a final statement deliniating how you will switch to holiness in order to make a difference, think creatively, and leverage your strengths and opportunities. Also, remember to mitigate or eliminate threats. Write your plan in the space below.

_____

_____

_____

_____

_____

_____

_____

_____

_____

_____

_____

_____

_____

_____

_____

_____

_____

_____

_____

Thank you for completing this workbook, and remember the following points as you launch to your destiny:

- *"Your current domain space and future sphere of influence are created by perceptions."*

- *"We can look into the rearview mirror and see what is behind us; hindsight gives a great view."*

- *"Space Language adds power to the conversation within the organization – speak up and be heard."*

- *"Launch your differences to make a difference."*

- *"After we are off the launch pad, we operate in an open space."*

- *"What gives lift should create alignment with personality and purpose"*

- *"Choose harmony and celebrate the power of personality and purpose each and every day. Others will begin to need and notice your extraordinary ways"*

ABOUT THE AUTHOR

Dr. Amanda H. Goodson

Goodson is a native of Decatur, Alabama and currently resides in Tucson, Arizona where God has entrusted her to serve as Pastor of Trinity Temple Christian Methodist Episcopal Church. She also plans and facilitates seminars, workshops, and retreats for the CME church.

She is President and on the Board of Directors for Never the Same Ministries (NTS), a God-inspired, Tucson based, Kingdom ministry dedicated to serve as a vessel through which people are provided tools and resources to develop a more spiritually mature and improved relationship with God through Christ. The NTS God ordered mission is to provide biblically based instruction, tools, and coaching for people within the community through planning and deployment of conferences and events across the United States.

God has gifted Goodson to be a Spirit-led preacher, teacher, trainer and coach for churches, agencies and non-profit organizations. Goodson connects with her audiences by sharing the Word of God through real-life experiences. She gives God glory as He allows her to inspire others to learn more about being a Spirit-led Christian in the world today. God has blessed her with an enthusiastic, energized and interactive method.

Goodson is fully committed to the Lord and knows that she has a blessed Spirit-led life. Her purpose is to fill the earth with the knowledge of God's glory by serving the Lord boldly through her ministry; bringing others closer to Christ and introducing Christ to those who have not accepted Him as their personal Savior. God's Word is her authority. Goodson believes that God's presence and power is Almighty and worthy to be praised. Further, she knows that God will make great things happen through His people.

Amanda has a Bachelor of Science in Electrical Engineering from Tuskegee University, a Master of Science in Management from Florida Institute of Technology, and a Doctor of Ministry from United Theological Seminary specializing in church administration.

As a Kingdom citizen, she is fully submitted to the will of God. Her prayer is to be active in sharing her faith, to make her thoughts agreeable to the will of God, and to have the mind of Christ. The Word of God is the final authority in her life.

Books by Dr. Amanda Goodson

Spiritual Quickbooks ™
Kingdom Character
Spiritual Authority
Carmel Voices
The Power to Make an Impact
Powerful People Follow Christ
Step out in Faith
Going Higher, Declarations for Kids
On the Rise
Spiritual Intelligence
Shift to Holiness

Leadership Minibooks ™
The Authority of a Leader
Character of a Leader
Unlock Your Full Potential
12 Power Principles for Administrative Professionals
Soar to Your Destiny

Leadership Workbooks
Unlock Your Full Potential Workbook

Cover design by Noah Paul